Original title:
Under Water

Editor: Theodor Taimla
Author: Marlen Vesiroos
ISBN HARDBACK: 978-9916-87-088-4
ISBN PAPERBACK: 978-9916-87-089-1

Lost in the Blue

Underneath the endless sky,
A whisper floats on waves nearby.
Silent dreams and shadows play,
Lost in hues where echoes stay.

Blue horizons stretch and sway,
Time slips gently, drifts away.
In the depths, a heart beats slow,
Finding peace in undertow.

Bubbles dance in sunlit beams,
Carried forth by whispered dreams.
A tranquil pulse, serene and true,
In this world of endless blue.

Siren's Serenade

Echoes call from rocky shores,
Siren songs and ocean roars.
Melodies of night and tide,
Draw me in, so deep, so wide.

Voices linger on the breeze,
Swaying softly through the trees.
Beneath the stars, my heart takes flight,
Captured by the moonlit night.

Waves entwine, a sweet embrace,
A haunting tune, a timeless grace.
In their depths, my spirit glides,
In the dance where magic hides.

Coral Chorus

In the reef, colors merge and flow,
Whispers of the deep, they glow.
Coral blooms in vibrant sway,
Singing songs of life's ballet.

Fins that flick and tails that twirl,
In this wonder, shells unfurl.
Harmony in every hue,
Nature's canvas, pure and true.

A gentle pulse beneath the waves,
Cradled in the ocean's caves.
Where each note and rhythm thrive,
Bringing forth a world alive.

The Gentle Pressure

Underneath the calming tide,
Softly whispers, waves abide.
Pressure builds, yet feels so light,
Cradled close, a sweet delight.

Floating in the ocean's arms,
Where the heart's beat softly calms.
Endless depths, yet ever near,
Wrapped in warmth, devoid of fear.

Every moment, fluid grace,
Time stays still in this embrace.
With each breath, a pulse, a sigh,
Down below, where dreams won't die.

Beneath the Waves

Beneath the waves, where silence dwells,
Secrets of the ocean swell.
Whispers dance in currents' flow,
Ancient tales that ebb and glow.

Coral gardens, colors bright,
Creatures lurking, out of sight.
A world alive, yet still and deep,
In shadows where the mermaids sleep.

Echoes of the tide's sweet song,
Links of time where dreams belong.
Starlit paths in azure haze,
Lost in the depths of ocean's maze.

Beneath the waves, a treasure lies,
In hidden caves, beneath blue skies.
A universe in each small shell,
In every wave, a story to tell.

Hidden Realms

Hidden realms, where magic flows,
In the forest, where no one goes.
Faint glimmers guide the way,
Through tangled roots, where fairies play.

In twilight's hush, the secrets bloom,
With whispers sweet, dispelling gloom.
Glimmers of light in shaded glades,
A dance of shadows, a serenade.

Beneath the boughs, enchantments weave,
Old spirits calling, inviting to believe.
The air is thick with mystery rare,
In hidden realms, find magic there.

Where every step brings tales anew,
In vibrant hues, the world imbues.
A canvas painted with nature's hand,
To wander here is to understand.

Luminous Depths

Luminous depths, where colors blend,
A world transformed, where shadows bend.
Bioluminescent glows ignite,
In the stillness of the night.

Creatures drift in gentle grace,
In this quiet, secret space.
Echoes shimmer as they rise,
Lighting dreams beneath dark skies.

A pulse of life, a heartbeat's song,
In depths where the brave belong.
Mysteries wrapped in swirling light,
In luminous depths, the heart takes flight.

A tapestry of stars below,
In whispers soft, the tides bestow.
An underwater paradise,
In every corner, wonder lies.

The Murmuring Sea

The murmuring sea calls out to me,
With stories lost from times carefree.
Waves that sigh, then wander far,
A lullaby from a distant star.

Footprints fade on sandy shores,
While shells remain, with deep-sea roars.
In the breeze, a tale unfolds,
Of sunken ships and treasures bold.

Sailboats dance on the water's crest,
As gulls overhead find their rest.
The whispers weave of salt and foam,
A promise of adventure's home.

As twilight paints the sky with fire,
The sea ignites a lost desire.
In every wave, a heartbeat clear,
The murmuring sea, forever near.

The Lure of Blue

In depths where secrets hide,
The ocean's heart beats slow.
A tranquil shade so wide,
It beckons us below.

With waves that whisper dreams,
And currents soft and sweet,
A dance of sunlit gleams,
Our journey's bittersweet.

The azure calls to roam,
To chase the playful tide.
In liquid shades we foam,
Our spirits open wide.

Yet in this endless sea,
A cautionary tale,
For beauty can't be free,
And sailors sometimes fail.

But still, we dive and swim,
Embracing waves of fate.
The lure of blue within,
An urge we can't negate.

Shadows in the Reef

Beneath the sunny glare,
A world of colors bloom.
Where shadows linger near,
And secrets find their room.

Coral castles stand tall,
Guardians of the deep.
In silence they enthrall,
Where fish and wonders leap.

A dance of light and shade,
The currents twist and twine.
In twilight's soft parade,
The mysteries entwine.

Yet danger hides within,
In beauty's sweet disguise.
A fate we may begin,
With peril in our eyes.

So wander through the blue,
With caution and a dream,
For shadows tell a tale,
In the reef's silent gleam.

Mysteries Beneath

In shadows deep, where secrets lay,
The whispers call, night turns to day.
Ancient tales in silence spun,
Beneath the waves, the lost will run.

Phantom ships of ages past,
Their haunting forms, too great to last.
With every tide, new stories rise,
Enigmas wrapped in ocean sighs.

Siren's Call

A lullaby in waves,
That echoes through the night.
With voices sweet yet grave,
They pull with all their might.

On rocks the waters crash,
With melodies of dream.
Enticing hearts to thrash,
In treacherous moonbeam.

The sirens weave their song,
In whispers soft and sly.
To follow feels so wrong,
Yet still we long to try.

With every note we drown,
In longing and in pain.
The beauty wears a crown,
Of sorrow, yet we gain.

So when the waves resound,
Hold fast, let not the lure
Of sirens' song surround,
For safety, we must ensure.

Aquatic Veins

Rivers twist through earth's embrace,
Crimson hues in liquid lace.
Fish like silver darts do weave,
In currents strong, they won't deceive.

Fragile life within each pool,
Nature's art, both wild and cruel.
From depths below to skies above,
Aquatic veins, a tale of love.

Veils of the Ocean

In veils of mist and foam,
The ocean's whispers flow.
A longing to call home,
In depths we cannot know.

Each wave a tale unraveled,
A story yet to tell.
In currents softly traveled,
We ride the ocean's swell.

With echoes in the spray,
The past and present blend.
Through time we drift away,
On journeys without end.

Yet in this fluid realm,
A power fierce and vast.
The ocean's steady helm,
Holds memories of the past.

So let the veils unfold,
And guide us through the blue.
For in the depths of gold,
The ocean calls us true.

The Aquatic Lullaby

Soft waves cradle the sleeping shore,
Moonlight dances on waters that soar.
Gentle whispers from the depths below,
Nature's hymn, a soothing flow.

Coral dreams in a vibrant hue,
Fish dart past, in a shimmering view.
Starfish twirl in their tranquil waltz,
While seaweed sways without a fault.

Seashells sing of tales untold,
Timeless secrets, treasures of gold.
The ocean rocks in a sweet embrace,
Caressing hearts in this sacred space.

Beneath the waves, a calm doth stay,
In the moon's glow, night hours play.
The aquatic lullaby softly calls,
Bringing peace as each heartbeat falls.

Sleep, dear child, to this serenade,
For in the water, dreams are made.
Close your eyes while the tides weep,
To the sound of the ocean's deep.

Dances of the Deep Blue

In the silence where shadows glide,
Creatures twirl in the ocean's tide.
A ballet played on a watery stage,
A dance of life, from age to age.

Octopuses stretch with graceful arms,
Embracing the rhythm of silent charms.
Schools of fish in a shimmering cloud,
Whirl and pirouette, joyful and loud.

Kelp forests sway to an ancient song,
Inviting all to dance along.
Crabs scuttle to their own beat,
While dolphins leap with nimble feet.

This vibrant life beneath the blue,
Holds secrets unknown to me and you.
Each movement tells a story bright,
A choreography of pure delight.

As currents flow, the dancers twine,
And stars above begin to shine.
In this grand ball of the ocean's lore,
The deep blue dances forevermore.

Echoes of the Sea

Whispers travel on ocean's breath,
Carrying tales of life and death.
Echoes rise from the depths below,
In rhythms soft, like waves that flow.

The call of gulls, a distant cheer,
Brings memories of those held dear.
Secrets murmur in salty air,
Beneath the surface lies the fare.

In the still of night when the world is mute,
The sea sings softly, a sacred flute.
With every wave, a story spun,
The echoes linger, one by one.

From shipwrecked dreams to lighthouse beams,
The ocean cradles our hopes and seams.
Her voice, a blanket, wraps us tight,
Guiding lost souls through dark and light.

So listen close to the ocean's plea,
In its vastness, we find the key.
Echoes of the sea ever remain,
A symphony of peace amid the pain.

Abyssal Ballad

In the deep where sunlight fades,
Darkness reigns and silence pervades.
Creatures lurk in the shadows deep,
Guarding secrets their hearts keep.

The weight of water, a heavy shroud,
Whispers hidden beneath the cloud.
Lonely melodies rise and fall,
An abyssal ballad, a haunting call.

Bioluminescence sparkles bright,
A dance of colors in the night.
Strange beings glide through waters cold,
Each a story, each a fold.

Time stands still in this hushed embrace,
As life unfolds at a different pace.
Resilient souls in the dark do sway,
An ancient rhythm, forever play.

So dive into the depths of dreams,
Where the silent ballad softly gleams.
For in the abyss, our souls unite,
In the darkest waters, we find our light.

Refuge Beneath the Waves

Coral gardens, colors bright,
Home to creatures, a pure delight.
In tranquil depths, they dance and sway,
A sanctuary, far from the fray.

The gentle hum of life abounds,
In silent realms, where peace resounds.
In the heart of blue, they thrive,
Refuge found, where dreams arrive.

Drifting in Stillness

Beneath the calm and quiet blue,
A world unfolds, so vast and true.
Gentle currents whisper low,
As time itself begins to slow.

Soft shadows dance in muted light,
As dreams weave through the endless night.
A stillness wraps the wandering mind,
Where peace and silence are entwined.

Drifting softly, lost in thought,
In this embrace, all worries caught.
The heart beats slow, the spirit free,
In perfect sync with the deep sea.

Floating gently, thoughts like foam,
In this quiet, I find my home.
Every wave a silent prayer,
In the deep, I breathe the air.

The vast expanse, an easy sigh,
As clouds above begin to fly.
In stillness, find the beating grace,
A moment held, a soft embrace.

Tales of the Ocean Floor

Beneath the waves, where secrets dwell,
The ocean floor has stories to tell.
Coral castles, vibrant and bright,
Guarded by shadows, lost to night.

Whispers of shells in the sand's embrace,
Tell of journeys in this vast space.
Echoes of laughter, glimmers of gold,
Each tale a treasure, waiting to unfold.

Anemones sway, in rhythm they dance,
In their world, life takes a chance.
The pulse of the ocean, a heartbeat below,
Each ripple a story, a soft ebb and flow.

Creatures of wonder, both strange and grand,
Roam the depths of this mystical land.
From giant squid to tiny shrimp,
In each tale, the shadows limply limp.

In the silence, magic takes flight,
With every glance, a glimmer of light.
The ocean floor, forevermore,
Keeps its tales in endless store.

Lighthouses of the Sea

Standing tall against the storm,
Guiding ships, their safety sworn.
With lanterns bright, they pierce the night,
A beacon's heart, a sailor's light.

Waves crash fierce against the stone,
Guardians of the waters lone.
With every dawn, their watch renews,
Whispers of hope, a seafarer's muse.

The Realm of Fish

In waters deep, where colors blend,
The realm of fish seems to transcend.
Glistening scales, a flash of grace,
Each creature holds a sacred space.

They swim with ease, a fluid form,
In schools they dance, through currents warm.
A ballet performed in endless flow,
In this realm, the heart will know.

Gentle giants glide through the sea,
While minnows flit so joyfully.
A world alive in every shade,
In the depths, all fears do fade.

Following whispers of ancient lore,
Where time forgets, forevermore.
The currents carry their silent song,
In the realm of fish, we all belong.

In shimmering light, they drift and play,
Each moment spent, a fleeting ballet.
With grace they teach, a tranquil dance,
In their realm, we find our chance.

Chasing Light in the Deep

Diving below, where shadows creep,
I search for light in the depths so steep.
A flicker here, a shimmer there,
In the dark, I catch my stare.

The sun's warmth fades, replaced by night,
Guided by dreams, I chase the light.
Bioluminescence, colors pure,
Offer hope in the dark, reassure.

Fish glow softly as they drift and sway,
Painting the ocean in luminous play.
Each pulse of life illuminates the dark,
A dance of creatures in the silent park.

In this world of muted hues,
I find the strength to chase, to choose.
The spark of life, a beacon bright,
In the depths, I am ignited by light.

With every breath, the ocean sings,
Chasing light, the heart takes wings.
Through shadowed waters, dreams take flight,
In the deep, I find my light.

Celestial Depths

In the silent, starry night,
An ocean deep with dreams in sight.
Ripples dance with a gentle grace,
Whispers echoed in time and space.

Waves embrace the glowing tide,
Stories hidden, time does hide.
Each flicker tells of journeys grand,
Amongst the pearls of silver sand.

Creatures glide in liquid flight,
Casting shadows, a mysterious light.
Colors swirl in a cosmic play,
Endless depths where silence sways.

Underneath the moon's soft glow,
Nature's secrets begin to flow.
A universe beneath the sea,
In celestial depths, wild and free.

Secrets of the Plankton

In shadows cast by gentle waves,
Tiny wonders in silence saves.
Drifters floating in a dance,
Secrets hidden in their chance.

Micro worlds in twilight creep,
In ocean's cradle, secrets sleep.
Each flicker a story, each swirl a clue,
Whispers of life in vibrant hue.

Feasting 'neath the surface light,
Life that ebbs and flows in flight.
Mysteries wrapped in a fragile shell,
The tales of plankton, who weave and dwell.

From darkness blooms an ancient lore,
In stillness, they quietly explore.
Gardens woven of glistening thread,
In the secrets of the plankton, life is fed.

Dance of the Jellyfish

In the ocean's grace, they float,
Dancing to a silent quote.
Tentacles twirl in fluid art,
A ballet lost, yet set apart.

Drifting through the azure waves,
Nature's rhythm softly braves.
With every pulse, they tell their tale,
In currents deep, where dreams prevail.

A glow of lanterns low and bright,
Lighting paths in the velvet night.
Cotton clouds of translucent fate,
In the dance of jellyfish, hearts elate.

Swirling colors, ethereal grace,
In fleeting beauty, they find their place.
With every drift, a story flows,
In the depths, where wonder grows.

Voices of the Nautilus

In chambers wrapped in ancient shell,
The nautilus begins to dwell.
Whispers echo through the tide,
In spiral paths, secrets abide.

Voices from the ocean's past,
In stories deep, forever cast.
With each heartbeat, life unfolds,
In liquid tales of the boldest holds.

Navigators of the deep cold blue,
Where mysteries arise, old and new.
Gentle giants of the sea,
In their depths, we find the key.

With every swirl in the silent night,
They speak of worlds bathed in light.
Timeless echoes in every groove,
In the voices of the nautilus, we move.

The Colors of Abyss

Deep shadows weave through the dark,
Hints of blue dance and spark.
Crimson whispers, silent yet loud,
In the heart of the void, so proud.

Violet echoes in twilight's shroud,
Emerald dreams beneath the crowd.
Each hue a tale, each shade a song,
That beckons the lost to come along.

Golden glimmers, fleeting and rare,
Secrets hidden in the cold air.
Silver threads of starlit grace,
Entwine the wanderer's face.

In this abyss where shadows play,
Colors collide, night meets day.
A canvas rich with stories untold,
Where the brave hearts gather bold.

Each breath a color, each heartbeat a blend,
In the abyss, the journeys ascend.
Embrace the chaos, let it unfurl,
In the colors of this dark, vast world.

Tidal Symphony

Waves whisper secrets to the shore,
In harmony, they rise and fall.
The ocean sings a timeless score,
Where echoes dance and waters call.

Moonlit tides in silvered glow,
Caress the sands with soft delight.
Every swell a tale of woe,
Every crash ignites the night.

Seagulls cry, a soaring refrain,
As currents weave their mystic thread.
The pulse of oceans, wild and unchained,
In rhythmic motion, endlessly spread.

Lighthouses stand, brave in the mist,
Guiding sailors back to the light.
In the tidal waves, dreams persist,
A symphony born of day and night.

Deep beneath where shadows dwell,
Mysteries swirl, unseen embrace.
In this watery world, spirits swell,
In the tidal symphony, find your place.

Fluid Fantasies

In liquid dreams, we drift and sway,
A canvas painted, bright and free.
Colors blend, then fade away,
Waves of thought, a reverie.

Streams of vision, so serene,
Flowing, swirling in gentle arcs.
Imagination's boundless sheen,
Where every ripple leaves a mark.

Beneath the surface, wonders thrive,
Shapes and forms, in motion, play.
In fluid realms, we come alive,
While reality slips away.

The dance of water, pure and light,
A symphony of whispers swell.
In this realm of dreams at night,
Every heartbeat casts a spell.

A journey into depths unknown,
Embrace the current, let it steer.
In fluid fantasies, we've grown,
To find the truth we hold so dear.

Silence of the Depths

In the stillness, shadows creep,
Where secrets lie in the ocean's keep.
A haunting murmur, soft as breath,
Echoes linger, dance with death.

Golden silence, thick as night,
Wraps the depths in ghostly light.
Every heartbeat, pulse so slow,
In this abyss where lost souls go.

Crystalline waters, dark and deep,
Hold the whispers of dreams we keep.
In this silence, memories fade,
An eternal pact, unafraid.

A gentle current tugs at fate,
As shadows weave and spirits wait.
The depth of night, profound and still,
Where silence reigns with quiet will.

Within this calm, the world feels vast,
Every sorrow, every joy, amassed.
In the silence of the depths, we find,
A reflection true, a heart entwined.

Ascend from the Depth

From shadows deep, where whispers dwell,
A journey starts, a silent bell.
With every rise, the light anew,
In strength we find, the path we pursue.

Through currents strong, and tides that sway,
We learn to fight, not drift away.
Our spirits lift, like sails unfurled,
To greet the dawn, to face the world.

Mountains high, we dare to climb,
Each step we take, a touch of time.
With faith as wings, we soar above,
The heart ignites, a flame of love.

In depths we forged the bonds that bind,
With every trial, the soul refined.
Together strong, we break the chain,
Ascend anew, transcending pain.

So here we stand, on heights so grand,
With dreams in hand, united we stand.
Through every storm, we've made our way,
Ascend from depth, to light of day.

The Blue Horizon

Beyond the waves, a canvas wide,
Where sea and sky in colors glide.
A dance of blue, a tranquil sea,
Calls every wanderer to be free.

The sun dips low, a golden hue,
Whispers soft, old tales renew.
Each breath a hymn, each glance a vow,
To chase the dreams, to live the now.

With horizons broad, our spirits soar,
Upon the breeze, we yearn for more.
In every glance, the vast unknown,
A place where hearts can find their own.

As dusk descends, the stars ignite,
A world awash in velvet night.
In every wave, a story told,
Of journeys taken, brave and bold.

The blue horizon, softly calls,
As waves embrace, and sunset falls.
With open hearts, we trust the tide,
In every heartbeat, we confide.

Reflections of the Unknown

In shadows cast, where secrets hide,
We seek the truths that lie inside.
Each echo whispers, a tender plea,
To face the fears, embrace the sea.

Mirrors show what's deep within,
A journey starts where we begin.
With every glance, the past unfolds,
In every heart, the story holds.

In silence kept, the mind will roam,
Through winding paths, we find our home.
The unknown waits with arms so wide,
A guiding light, we shall not bide.

Each step we take, a tale to weave,
In every sorrow, we learn to grieve.
Reflections spark, the heart finds grace,
In shadows deep, we find our place.

So venture forth, explore the night,
Where every doubt can turn to light.
In whispers soft, the truth we'll find,
Reflections call us, unconfined.

Beneath the Foam

Beneath the foam, where whispers sway,
The sea conceals what it can't say.
In depths so dark, the mysteries sleep,
A world alive, the secrets keep.

The tides they pull, the currents lead,
To treasures found, in dreams we heed.
In shimmering light, the shadows dance,
Awakening hope, a second chance.

Each shell a story, each wave a song,
In nature's heart, we all belong.
With every splash, the past flows free,
The ocean's depth, a symphony.

Through rolling waves, we drift and glide,
In every swell, the heart confides.
Beneath the foam, a realm untold,
Where spirits brave, and dreams unfold.

So let us dive, the journey starts,
In waters deep, we share our hearts.
With open minds, the sea we roam,
Together we'll find our way back home.

Depths of Discovery

In shadows deep, where secrets lie,
A world unfolds beneath the sky.
With every turn, a story found,
In ancient depths, where dreams abound.

Mysteries swirl in currents wide,
As whispers of the ocean glide.
Explorers brave, with hearts so bold,
Unravel tales the waves have told.

Beyond the foam, where silence reigns,
A treasure trove of uncharted plains.
With every dive, the heart awakes,
In hidden realms, the spirit shakes.

Lights dance softly, in beats and flows,
What wonders hide, no one truly knows.
A journey vast, with no set course,
The sea becomes our guiding force.

From depths we rise, our spirits soar,
With every wave, we seek for more.
In salty air, the truth we seek,
In depths of discovery, we speak.

Sirens of the Deep

In ocean's swell, the sirens sing,
Their melodies in the water cling.
With haunting notes, they call us near,
To realms unknown, both bright and sheer.

Softly they beckon, with shimmering light,
A dance that twirls through day and night.
But hidden dangers, beneath the song,
In depths of beauty, we can't belong.

Lured by their charm, we drift so low,
Into a dream where shadows grow.
Yet wisdom whispers through the tide,
To heed the waves and bide our pride.

Their laughter echoes, a watery chime,
Entwined with love, yet lost in time.
Mysteries weave through the salt-kissed air,
A paradox of joy and despair.

With caution we tread, on this fragile seam,
For the sirens' call is but a dream.
In depths of wonder, we find our way,
Yet remember, the tides may sway.

Beneath Celestial Waters

Beneath the waves, stars softly gleam,
A tranquil world, like a whispered dream.
In the dark, where secrets thrive,
The cosmic dance keeps hope alive.

Moonlit paths, where the fishes glide,
In liquid realms, where time can't hide.
Each ripple stirs a memory deep,
Of ancient tales, our hearts must keep.

Here, silence reigns, a soothing balm,
In tranquil depths, the soul feels calm.
A symphony of tides and swells,
In harmony with the ocean's bells.

Among the corals, life takes flight,
Colors blend in the fading light.
A tapestry woven in the depths,
Each thread entwined, with nature's depths.

As twilight falls, we drift and sway,
In this embrace, we long to stay.
Beneath celestial waters so grand,
We find our peace, heart in hand.

Twilight beneath the Tide

Twilight glows where the waters meet,
A dance of shadows, soft and sweet.
The horizon whispers tales of old,
In hues of amber and marigold.

Beneath the tide, dreams intertwine,
With starlit paths, where hearts align.
The gentle waves caress the shore,
A lullaby that calls for more.

With every breath, the ocean sighs,
Secrets hidden, where silence lies.
In twilight moments, magic brews,
As the day's colors softly fuse.

Night descends, with a velvet cloak,
In watery depths, the world awoke.
Here, we linger, lost in time,
Dancing with rhythm, sweet as rhyme.

So let us glide through this serene,
In twilight's embrace, where we have been.
With whispers of waves, and laughter bright,
We savor the joy of night's pure light.

Boundless Below

In the depths where silence reigns,
The whispers of the ocean lanes,
Life dances in a cosmic sigh,
Boundless dreams in layers lie.

Corals bloom like jeweled skies,
In currents deep, the secret lies,
Creatures roam with graceful peace,
A symphony that will not cease.

The shadows play in twilight's grace,
Each curve reveals a hidden face,
Wonders weave an endless tale,
As time drifts softly like a sail.

Glowing orbs in water's light,
Mark the journey through the night,
In silence, stories intertwine,
Boundless beauty, yours and mine.

So dive into the liquid deep,
Where memories and secrets sleep,
The ocean's heart will always glow,
And tell the tales of boundless below.

The Spirits of the Reef

Beneath the waves, where shadows play,
The spirits of the reef sway,
In colors bright, they weave their song,
A dance of life where hearts belong.

Soft whispers ride the ocean's breath,
Echoes of life, beyond the death,
Coral castles, ancient and bright,
Guarding tales of day and night.

Each flicker tells of love and loss,
In tidal tales, they find their gloss,
A world alive, so fragile, free,
In harmony, they sing with glee.

From tiny fish to giants bold,
The stories of the reef unfold,
Connected by a sacred thread,
Where every heartbeat's gently fed.

So let us cherish, and not betray,
The spirits of the reef today,
For in their dance, we see the light,
A hymn to life, forever bright.

Stories in Sea Glass

Strewn upon the sandy shore,
Fragments whisper tales of yore,
Each piece a memory polished bright,
Stories twinkling in the light.

Once vessels crossed the vast blue seas,
Now in silence, they catch the breeze,
Colorful shards of past delight,
Reflecting dreams in morning light.

As tides reclaim what once was lost,
Each shiny gem bears witness, tossed,
To journeys sailed, both calm and wild,
Echoes cherished, forever compiled.

In the wind's soft, gentle call,
The stories rise and softly fall,
A mosaic of the heart's embrace,
Life's canvas captured in sea glass space.

So gather the pieces from the land,
Feel the past within your hand,
For every shard that gleams and sways,
Holds the essence of bygone days.

Chasing Shadows in the Waves

Upon the surf, where shadows play,
We chase the dusk, we seek the day,
In every splash, a moment's glee,
Our laughter dancing wild and free.

The sun dips low, the horizon glows,
As night's embrace gently bestows,
An echo of the day's farewell,
While secrets of the deep swell.

With feet in foam, we wade along,
A melody of dusk's sweet song,
The ripples whisper what's to come,
In twilight's arms, we feel at home.

Through vibrant hues of dusk's soft sighs,
We find our dreams in painted skies,
Each pulse of wave, each rush of tide,
Draws us closer, side by side.

So let us chase the shadows near,
In the embrace of salt and cheer,
For in the waves, our spirits soar,
Chasing shadows forevermore.

Rippled Secrets

In the quiet pond, whispers dwell,
Beneath the surface, stories tell.
Waves that shimmer, softly sway,
Holding secrets of the day.

Fish dart in a graceful dance,
Caught in a fleeting chance.
From the shadows, dreams escape,
In the water's gentle shape.

A breeze stirs the hidden lore,
Of ancient tides, forevermore.
Ripples spread with every sigh,
Carrying truths that never die.

As the evening sun descends,
Nature's rhythm softly bends.
In these depths, the heart can sink,
Finding solace in the brink.

With each ripple, thoughts unfold,
Whispers of the brave and bold.
Here in silence, bonds are made,
In the water's cool cascade.

The Gold of the Ocean

Waves crash down on sunlit shores,
Glistening treasures, nature's stores.
Seashells scattered, gems of light,
Calling sailors through the night.

The horizon stretches, vast and grand,
Where skies and sea meet, hand in hand.
Golden sunsets fade to blue,
Painting dreams both bold and true.

In the depths, the riches lie,
Waiting for the brave to try.
Courage dwells in every heart,
As tides of change begin to part.

Fishermen cast their nets with care,
Hopes reflected in the air.
With every catch, stories weave,
Of all the journeys they believe.

The ocean holds its timeless gold,
A legacy yet to unfold.
With each wave, a promise made,
In the dance of light and shade.

Harbors of Mystery

In the mist, where shadows play,
Harbors whisper night and day.
Boats gently rock in hidden slips,
Carving tales on sailing trips.

Lanterns flicker, guiding home,
Spirits wander, never alone.
Shorelines echo with soft sighs,
Secret love, beneath the skies.

In these corners, dreams collide,
Rippling water, secrets hide.
Every wave a tale untold,
Mysteries in the night unfold.

Salted air carries the past,
Fleeting moments that never last.
Glimmers fade with morning light,
Leaving shadows in the night.

Harbors calm with endless grace,
Holding stories, time can't erase.
In their depths, a world to see,
Awaits the heart, so wild and free.

Moonlit Depths

Beneath the moon's soft, silver glow,
The ocean stirs, a gentle flow.
Whispers rise from foamy waves,
Carrying dreams of hidden graves.

Stars reflect on waters deep,
Secrets guarded, theirs to keep.
In the silence, echoes roam,
Guiding lost souls safely home.

With every tide, a story swells,
Of ancient ships and ringing bells.
The night unfolds with every crest,
Gifts of wisdom in their rest.

A lullaby from depths below,
As shadows dance in moonlit show.
Magic weaves through every hue,
Bringing wonders yet to view.

In this realm where silence speaks,
And hidden wonders gently peek,
Moonlit depths, a siren's song,
Calls to hearts where they belong.

Dancing with the Tides

The waves rise high, a rhythmic play,
They twist and turn, in gentle sway.
Salted breezes kiss the shore,
In every splash, I crave for more.

Footprints fade in shifting sand,
Each moment lost, a fleeting hand.
Underneath the vast sky's dome,
The ocean's heartbeat feels like home.

Colors blend, the sunset glows,
With every pulse, the ocean flows.
I twirl with joy, I leap and glide,
In this embrace, I dance with tides.

Seagulls cry, they echo free,
Waves whisper tales to you and me.
Together we'll waltz 'neath the stars,
In harmony, without any bars.

The night unveils its tranquil grace,
Reflecting light on water's face.
With every rise, with every fall,
I find my peace, I hear the call.

Currents of Silence

In quiet depths, the stillness sings,
Where shadows touch on whispered wings.
The ocean breathes a gentle sigh,
As time drifts slowly, passing by.

Beneath the waves, a secret world,
With dreams and thoughts so softly swirled.
Crystal waters cradle my fears,
In currents calm, lost amidst tears.

Each bubble speaks of hopes untold,
In silence warm, we feel the bold.
Secrets hidden in the flow,
Guide the heart where it must go.

As ripples dance beneath the moon,
A serenade, a soothing tune.
In the embrace of night's delight,
I find my soul, in soft twilight.

The echo fades, yet I remain,
In currents deep, I'll feel no pain.
With every breath, each silent wave,
I learn to love, I learn to save.

Depths of Serenity

In tranquil waters, peace unwinds,
Embracing all that calmness finds.
Below the surface, stillness reigns,
Where quiet hearts release their chains.

A gentle pulse, the sea's embrace,
Reflecting dreams in a soft grace.
Amidst the blue, I find my place,
In depths where time begins to chase.

Each starfish glistens, tells a tale,
Of journeys past and winds that sail.
In every tide, a lesson flows,
With every wave, my spirit grows.

Echoes linger, softly hum,
In vibrant hues, I'm overcome.
Where solitude is sweetly found,
In depths of peace, I'm tightly bound.

The water's song, a lullaby,
Beneath vast skies, I learn to fly.
With every dive, each stroke anew,
In serenity, I start anew.

Forgotten Treasures

On sandy shores, the stories lie,
Of sailors lost beneath the sky.
Each shell and stone, a memory,
In whispered winds, their legacy.

Forgotten maps in ocean blue,
Lead to wonders, deep and true.
The tides reclaim what time has tossed,
In every wave, the past is lost.

With each new dawn, we seek the light,
Uncovering dreams that hide from sight.
A treasure chest of hopes and fears,
Legacies woven through the years.

The salty breeze carries the lore,
Of journeys made, and those before.
Each find a spark, igniting fire,
In hearts anew, the deep desire.

So seek you now, the sands of old,
For every grain, a tale is told.
In forgotten treasures, truth is found,
In waves and whispers, love's profound.

Liquid Embrace

In the stillness of dawn's light,
Whispers flow like a gentle tide,
Each droplet cradles a dream,
Softly wrapped, where hopes reside.

The river sings to the cool stones,
Carving paths through the morning mist,
Where shadows dance on the surface,
A liquid embrace, a tender tryst.

Beneath the waves, secrets rustle,
Echoes of life weave through the foam,
A world submerged in its silence,
Home to the wanderer's roam.

Time drifts by in fluid motion,
As currents pull at the heart's core,
In this symphony of water,
We find what we are yearning for.

Lost in the depths, the soul sighs,
Cradled within the aqua hues,
Every splash a soft reminder,
Of the love that life imbues.

Coral Reveries

Beneath the sun's warm embrace,
Coral dreams bloom bright and free,
In a realm where colors mingle,
And whispers drift through the sea.

Each swirl tells a tale of wonder,
Of creatures dancing in delight,
A ballet amidst the formations,
Filled with mystery and light.

The tide carries tales of ages,
Secrets hidden in the swell,
Softened echoes of the ocean,
In this underwater citadel.

Seahorses sway in gentle rhythm,
As fish weave through coral lanes,
In this delicate tapestry,
Nature's art, where beauty reigns.

In coral reveries, we linger,
Pausing to admire the view,
For in this vibrant sanctuary,
Our hearts find solace anew.

Secrets of the Depths

Deep within where shadows slumber,
Lies a world of whispered lore,
Echoes of time trapped in silence,
Secrets hidden evermore.

The ocean cradles ancient stories,
In the sway of its gentle pull,
Legends etched within the silt,
In every dip and every lull.

Creatures glide through dim lit waters,
With grace that defies the light,
Guardians of the depths, they wander,
In realms shrouded from our sight.

Every bubble tells a secret,
An unsung melody of the deep,
Where mysteries blend with echoes,
And the ocean's heart must keep.

In stillness, we chase reflections,
Of souls that swim in depths profound,
For in the silence and shadows,
The meaning of life is found.

Currents of Solitude

In the quiet of the waters,
Souls drift softly, yet entwined,
With gentle currents that carry,
Thoughts of those they left behind.

Each wave a story, each ripple,
A whisper lost in the blue,
Where solitude finds a partner,
In the dance of me and you.

The sea, a vast and silent friend,
Embracing hearts that long to roam,
With every tide, a new beginning,
In currents that lead us home.

Through the depths of solitude's grasp,
We find solace in the flow,
A reminder that we're connected,
By the love that we bestow.

In the stillness, dreams awaken,
Guided by the moon's soft light,
Currents of solitude whisper,
In the quiet of the night.

The Ocean's Embrace

Waves crash upon the shore,
Whispers of the deep ocean's lore.
Salt in the air, a prayer sung,
Where tides dance and dreams are young.

Under the moon's gentle gaze,
Secrets held in watery haze.
The horizon stretches wide and free,
A heartbeat shared between you and me.

In hues of blue and turquoise bright,
Nature's canvas, a pure delight.
With every drop, my spirit sings,
In the ocean's arms, my heart takes wing.

Seagulls cry in the salty breeze,
A harmony that puts me at ease.
Drifting thoughts like ships at sail,
In the ocean's embrace, I shall prevail.

The sun dips low, a fiery glow,
Casting reflections in waves below.
With each sunset, my worries cease,
In the ocean's arms, I find my peace.

Webs of Seaweed

Underwater gardens sway and dance,
In tangled threads, a salty romance.
Seaweed whispers secrets near,
Of ocean worlds, both far and dear.

Bright greens and browns, a vibrant hue,
Living tapestries of ocean's view.
Crabs scuttle through their leafy homes,
Around each curve, adventure roams.

Tides pull gently, a rhythmic sway,
As creatures play in the sea's ballet.
Life intertwined in every strand,
A mystic woven by nature's hand.

Beneath the surface, the story grows,
Of strength and resilience that nature knows.
In gentle currents, freedom reigns,
In webs of seaweed, love remains.

Child of the tides, forever bound,
In the ocean's cradle, life is found.
Each wave tells tales, both old and new,
In this watery world, dreams come true.

Forgotten Sunlight

In shadows deep where silence lies,
A flicker of warmth beneath the skies.
Whispers of light in memories dwell,
Vivid stories too bright to tell.

Once golden rays kissed every shore,
Now they flicker, need to restore.
Ripples of time wash over the sea,
Forgotten sunlight calls out to me.

Echoes linger of laughter and play,
Fading reminders of a golden day.
In the ocean's heart, where brightness sleeps,
Awaits the dawn, where hope still creeps.

Glimmers dance upon the water's face,
Catching the dreams of time and space.
With every wave, stories revive,
In forgotten sunlight, we feel alive.

So let us walk where shadows blend,
And find the light that guides us to mend.
In the depths of dark, a promise gleams,
In forgotten sunlight, we find our dreams.

Below the Foam

A world beneath the frothy crest,
Where mysteries and whispers rest.
Creatures hide in the cool embrace,
In the depths, they find their space.

Anemones sway, soft and slow,
Their vibrant colors start to glow.
Bubbles rise in a gentle stream,
Below the foam, life's a dream.

Coral reefs like castles stand,
Gardens blooming in ocean's land.
Fish dart by in shimmering trails,
In this kingdom, adventure prevails.

The dances of currents, a lullaby,
Echoing secrets as they flow by.
In hidden realms where shadows play,
Beauty thrives in its own way.

So take a dive, explore the deep,
Embrace the wonders, secrets to keep.
For below the foam, life is profound,
In the heart of the sea, joy is found.

Moonlit Reflections

The moon hangs low, a silver hue,
Casting shadows, a tranquil view.
Whispers of night, softly they call,
Starlit secrets, enchanting all.

Ripples dance on the calm sea's face,
Each wave's journey, a gentle trace.
Eclipsed by dreams, the night holds tight,
Guiding our hearts through the velvet night.

In quiet corners, memories gleam,
Drifting on echoes of a fading dream.
The world asleep, yet we remain,
Bound by the glow, where love sustains.

With every breath, the night unfolds,
Stories of love and tales of old.
Moonlit reflections weave in the dark,
Illuminating paths, igniting a spark.

So let us wander, hand in hand,
Through vast horizons, across the sand.
In the dance of shadows, let souls align,
Under the moon, a love divine.

The Quiet Depth

Beneath the surface, stillness reigns,
Where mysteries hide and darkness chains.
Gentle whispers in the watery gloom,
Secrets linger in the ocean's tomb.

Down where the sunlight fades away,
Creatures drift in a silent ballet.
Time stands still in this hidden space,
Each heartbeat echoes with perfect grace.

Coral gardens bloom with colors bright,
Yet life remains tucked away from light.
In this realm, the shadows play,
Crafting stories in a subtle sway.

Here dreams entwine with the ebb and flow,
In the quiet depth, we learn to grow.
Whispers of ages, old and wise,
Guide us gently beneath the skies.

So let us dive into the serene,
And embrace wonders yet to be seen.
In the depths of the soul, we shall find,
A world of secrets entwined and blind.

Secrets of the Ocean Floor

In the blue abyss, the secrets lie,
Cradled gently by waves nearby.
Mysteries waiting to be unfurled,
Tales of the deep, a hidden world.

Tides that carry whispers untold,
Echoes of dreams as the waters unfold.
Curved shells glisten like stories sung,
In the heart of the sea, where life first sprung.

Ancient ruins, remnants of time,
Marking the stages in silence and rhyme.
Each grain of sand holds a piece of lore,
A fragment of life from the ocean floor.

Stars of the sea, both small and grand,
Leave an imprint upon the sand.
With every ripple and wave that break,
The ocean whispers of what's at stake.

So listen close to the watery song,
In the depths, we'll find where we belong.
Secrets entangled in currents flow,
Binding us gently to all we know.

Nautical Dreams

Sails unfurl in the morning light,
Each breeze carries dreams, taking flight.
Waves embrace the ship's rugged frame,
A journey awaited, calling our name.

Horizons beckon with whispers sweet,
As we chart our course, hearts skip a beat.
In every swell, adventure lies,
Under the endless, open skies.

Stars guide our path in the quiet dark,
Illuminating the seafarer's mark.
Nighttime tales of distant shores,
Unravel dreams behind closed doors.

The rhythm of water, the captain's song,
A melody where we all belong.
Crashing waves, a symphony grand,
Unites our spirits, a steady hand.

Through storms we sail and find our way,
With trust as our anchor, come what may.
Bound by the tides, we drift and roam,
In nautical dreams, we find our home.

Beneath the Swaying Seaweed

Hidden in the ocean's lap,
Where seaweed dances soft and slow,
Secrets whisper through the depths,
In emerald waves, the mysteries flow.

Creatures glide with grace untold,
In shadows cast by sun's warm gleam,
Bubbles rise like dreams afloat,
In the sea's embrace, we gently dream.

A current pulls, a gentle sigh,
Where currents weave the tales of old,
Life sways beneath the azure sky,
In depths where stories are retold.

The tide reveals what time forgets,
In tangled beds of soft sea grass,
Each sway a note in nature's fret,
As moments linger, fleet as glass.

Beneath the surface, calm and serene,
An underwater world takes flight,
In every wave, a tranquil sheen,
Beneath the sway, pure joy ignites.

The Drowning Whisper

In twilight's grasp, the oceans moan,
With secrets deep, like shadows cast,
A whisper calls from waves alone,
Of lovers lost, and time amassed.

The salty breeze carries a prayer,
For those who sink beneath the swell,
Echos ripple through the air,
In depths where countless stories dwell.

Beneath the stars, the waters churn,
In restless tides, the past will wade,
Each gentle wave, a heart that yearns,
In foamy dance, the grief cascades.

The moonlit path reflects despair,
With every swell, a silent plea,
Yet in the dark, love's flame burns bare,
A light enduring, wild and free.

So listen close to whispers low,
In the embrace of ocean's breath,
For in each tide, we find the flow,
Of life, of love, amidst the death.

Ocean's Embrace

In blue horizons, dreams collide,
As waves unfold their endless grace,
The ocean holds, a safe inside,
With every crest, a soft embrace.

Beneath the sun, the waters gleam,
Cradling time in rhythmic dance,
In tranquil currents, heartbeats dream,
Surrender to the sea's romance.

As shells whisper of tales untold,
Each grain of sand a moment's truth,
In tides of blue, both fierce and bold,
The ocean lends its bounteous youth.

In salty air, we breathe the past,
The waves return, then softly sway,
In ocean's arms, our souls are cast,
Infinite tides that bring the day.

With every wave, a breath is drawn,
In ocean's heart, we find our song,
Beneath the sky, at every dawn,
In ocean's arms, we all belong.

Tides of Time

As moonlight spills on waters wide,
The tides pull back, then rush to shore,
With every ebb, we bide our time,
In whispers loud, the ocean's lore.

Moments crash like waves in play,
Each high tide brings a brand new light,
In cycles deep, we find our way,
Through endless night, into the bright.

Time dances like the rolling foam,
In ceaseless rhythm, change unfolds,
The current runs towards distant home,
With stories woven, yet untold.

In fleeting waves, our memories rise,
A treasure trove of joy and tears,
Each tide a glimpse of lullabies,
In soft embrace, we cast our fears.

So let the ocean cradle time,
In every wave, a beat, a rhyme,
For in its depths, we intertwine,
In tides of love, we are sublime.

The Sea's Lament

The waves whisper tales, soft and low,
Of ships long lost, where few dare go.
Beneath the foam, secrets lie still,
Yearning for peace, a heart to fill.

Salt-tinged breezes carry the pain,
Echoes of sailors who danced with the rain.
Their laughter fades into the night,
A haunting song, a fleeting light.

Storm clouds gather, shadows entwine,
The sea's deep sorrow, a tear divine.
Each tide a memory, restless and bold,
Waves weave the stories that won't grow old.

Coral graves cradle their plight,
Crimson and gold in the fading light.
The sea's lament, a melody grand,
Sing us the secrets of your vast land.

Final goodbye to the voyage embraced,
To the dreams of sailors, forever graced.
In every splash, in every swell,
The sea's deep heart has much to tell.

Submerged Elegy

Beneath the waves, the silence screams,
Trapped in the shadows of broken dreams.
Ancient relics, stories entwined,
In watery graves, their fates aligned.

The depths conceal a lost refrain,
Echoes of joy, marred by the pain.
Sunken whispers float through the deep,
Where secrets of time are hidden to keep.

Corroded anchors of battles fought,
Lessons of courage that fate has taught.
The ocean holds what hearts can't see,
A song of loss, forever free.

Fish dance through the remnants past,
Life blooms softly, though shadows cast.
The beauty of loss, a paradox true,
In watery depths, life's cycle renews.

So if you wander where silence reigns,
Hear the submerged elegy that remains.
For every end is but a start,
In the ocean's depths, the echoes impart.

Veiled Wonders

Hidden treasures beneath the guise,
Veiled wonders swim past curious eyes.
Colors vibrant, creatures divine,
In the ocean's depths, they twinkle and shine.

Mysteries swirl in a dance of light,
Shadowy forms glide out of sight.
Glimmers of magic in every turn,
The sea's great tales forever burn.

Drifting softly, the currents weave,
Stories of light that few believe.
A fragile world with secrets to share,
Veiled wonders glimmer, beyond compare.

With every ripple, with every wave,
Life finds a way in the depths so grave.
In this realm of marvels, lost and free,
Echoes of magic, a symphony.

So dive headfirst, embrace the thrill,
Seek out the wonders, let your heart fill.
For in the ocean's depths, dreams come alive,
Veiled wonders await, where spirits thrive.

Beneath the Surface

Rippling waters conceal a world,
Where mysteries and marvels are unfurled.
A tapestry woven by nature's hand,
Beneath the surface, beauty will stand.

Hidden pathways of currents glide,
Where sea life dances in joyful pride.
Anemones sway in a gentle embrace,
Life flourishes deep in this silent space.

Glistening schools in choreographed flight,
Chasing the sun, casting silver light.
Every splash tells a story untold,
Of vibrant lives that would not fold.

So much beneath, so few to know,
The wonders that shimmer, the secrets that flow.
Each layer, a life, a moment to keep,
In the vast blue heart where silence sleeps.

Explore the depths, venture in deep,
Find solace where ancient shadows creep.
For beneath the surface, treasures reside,
A timeless dance, forever tied.

Veils of the Ocean

Whispers ride the salty air,
Secrets hidden deep and rare.
Waves that dance with moonlit gleam,
Veils of water, dreams that teem.

Coral gardens, colors bright,
Under currents, lost from sight.
Tides that rise and fall in time,
Rhythms flowing, soft as rhyme.

Mysterious shades in deep blue,
Echoes of the past we view.
Fins that flicker, shadows pass,
In this realm of fluid glass.

To the depths, a venture bold,
Stories waiting to be told.
With each plunge, find what we seek,
In the silence, hear it speak.

Veils that shimmer, call to me,
From the ocean's vast decree.
In its arms, I shall remain,
Bound by beauty, free of chain.

Depths of Desire

In the stillness, passion stirs,
Embers glowing, soft as purrs.
Whispers linger in the night,
Eyes that shimmer, hearts take flight.

Every glance a spark ignites,
As the yearning softly writes.
Words unspoken, yet they bind,
In their depths, our souls combined.

A dance of shadows, mere delight,
Lost in glances, burning bright.
In the silence, secrets share,
In the fragrance of your hair.

Threads of longing weave our fate,
Twisting softly, 'til too late.
In the pauses, time suspends,
As the world around us bends.

Depths of longing pull us near,
In this moment, hearts sincere.
Bound by fate, by whispered dreams,
In our essence, pure it seems.

Currents of Grace

Gentle breezes through the trees,
Carry whispers, soft as pleas.
Leaves that rustle, dance in tune,
With the rhythm, heart in swoon.

Sunlight dapples on the ground,
Nature's voice a soothing sound.
In the stillness, peace we find,
Open hearts and open mind.

Flowing rivers, timeless grace,
Every drop a warm embrace.
Winding paths, we glide along,
In the currents, life's sweet song.

With each moment, breathe it in,
Feel the joy that's deep within.
Through the struggles, through the strife,
Currents carry, full of life.

Embrace the beauty, let it flow,
In every heartbeat, let it grow.
Currents bind us, strong and true,
In their dance, I find you too.

Memories in Motion

Fleeting moments, shadows cast,
Time a river flowing fast.
In the echoes, laughter rings,
Every heartbeat softly sings.

Snapshots captured, colors flare,
Whispered secrets in the air.
Lost in thoughts, a tender glance,
In the dance of sweet romance.

Faces blur, but feelings stay,
Through the years, they guide our way.
Memories shimmer, bright as stars,
In our hearts, despite the scars.

As the seasons ebb and flow,
Life's a play, a grand tableau.
Moments treasured, wrapped in light,
Memories hold us through the night.

In the turning, find the grace,
Of the past we can't replace.
Every heartbeat, every sigh,
Memories in motion, never die.

Fathomless Echoes

In the depths where shadows play,
Whispers dance, drift away.
Silent screams, the heart does cry,
Beneath the waves, old memories lie.

Timeless tales in the blue expanse,
Lost in the depths, they swirl and prance.
Every ripple, a ghostly sound,
Fathomless echoes, forever bound.

The ocean's secrets, deep and vast,
Tales of shipwrecks, stories past.
Ceaseless tides, they ebb and flow,
In watery graves, lost dreams below.

Moonlight spills on the liquid night,
Casting shadows, ethereal light.
With every wave, the heart takes wing,
To the depths where the sirens sing.

In the solace of salty air,
Fathomless echoes, beyond compare.
Embrace the depths, let go of fear,
For in the abyss, love draws near.

Mirage of the Deep

Beneath the surface, visions play,
A mirage seen in the light of day.
Coral gardens, bright and fair,
Life and color, everywhere.

In quiet caverns, shadows creep,
Truth submerged, secrets deep.
Reflections tease the curious mind,
A path unwritten, yet to find.

Flickering forms in the ocean's sway,
Illusions shift and drift away.
The siren's call, a beckoning tune,
Beneath the waves, beneath the moon.

With every breath, reality bends,
What is real? Time contends.
Mirages shimmer, haunting, fair,
In the depths, a dream to share.

In the silence, a truth unfolds,
The ocean whispers, her stories told.
A tapestry woven, love and loss,
In the mirage, discover the cost.

Ocean's Pulse

Feel the rhythm, hear the tide,
Ocean's pulse, where secrets bide.
Every wave, a heartbeat strong,
In nature's symphony, we belong.

The ebb and flow, a dance so grand,
Echoing dreams on the soft, warm sand.
With every crash, a new refrain,
An endless cycle, joy and pain.

Currents whisper stories untold,
Adventures bold, treasures of gold.
A lover's touch in the salty air,
With every pulse, the world laid bare.

Drifting ships on horizons wide,
Trust the motion of the tide.
In the ocean's pulse, feel alive,
Where fleeting moments always thrive.

Dancing shadows beneath the foam,
In ocean's arms, we find our home.
The pulse of life, in every wave,
A soothing rhythm, strong and brave.

The Hidden World

Beneath the waves, a world concealed,
A vibrant realm, its fate revealed.
In coral halls, colors ignite,
A hidden wonder, pure delight.

Creatures dance in liquid grace,
Each a story, each a trace.
Anemones sway, fish dart by,
In the ocean's heart, they fly.

Caverns echo with whispered lore,
From ages past, forevermore.
A sanctuary, a quiet plea,
In every current, life runs free.

Light filters down in shimmering beams,
Filling the depths with vibrant dreams.
The hidden world sings its song,
Through every wave, we all belong.

Join the dance of the silent tide,
Find the magic where dreams abide.
In this realm, together we twirl,
Embracing the beauty of the hidden world.

The Ocean's Heartbeat

Waves whisper secrets, soft and deep,
Rhythmic pulses, where shadows creep,
Moonlight dances on shimmering waves,
The ocean sings of lost sailors' graves.

Beneath the surface, life connects,
Anemones sway as the current reflects,
Creatures glide, in a silent embrace,
Each heartbeat echoes in this sacred space.

Stars above twinkle in twilight's hue,
Colorful fish swim, in waters so blue,
Giant whales call, in a song from the past,
The ocean's heartbeat, forever vast.

Tides rise and fall, a constant ballet,
Shells in the sand tell stories of play,
Nature's rhythm, both fierce and sweet,
In every wave, our hearts skip a beat.

So listen closely to the sea's soft sighs,
In her vast depths, all wonder lies,
For in the ocean, both treasure and art,
Lies the eternal, the ocean's heartbeat.

Beneath the Tide

Dancing reflections in the light,
Beneath the waves, there's life in sight.
Creatures roam in a world so wide,
Secrets held beneath the tide.

Coral reefs painted bright and bold,
A tapestry of stories untold,
Fish dart swiftly, a flash of grace,
In this hidden, vibrant space.

The sea floor whispers tales of old,
Shipwrecks rest, their memories cold,
Barnacles cling, time's gentle hand,
Life persists in this sacred land.

Tides ebb away, then rush back fast,
Moments cherished, forever to last,
The ocean's pulse, a steady guide,
Beneath the waves, where dreams abide.

Listen to the whispers of the deep,
Beneath the tide, secrets we keep,
Life unfolds in a rhythmic weave,
In the silent depths, we believe.

The Twilight Zone

In the fading light of day,
The ocean stirs in a dreamlike sway,
Colors blend as shadows play,
In the twilight zone, we drift away.

Underwater forests, swaying slowly,
A dance of life, unspoken, holy,
Eels peek out with curious eyes,
In this twilight, where magic lies.

Soft-shelled creatures crawl with care,
A vibrant world waits, beyond compare,
As the sun sinks, the calm prevails,
In the twilight zone, the mystery sails.

Fluorescent fish flicker and glow,
Guided by currents, an ebb and flow,
Each gentle wave a soft caress,
In the twilight, we find our rest.

Here in the silence, time drifts away,
The ocean whispers, night turning to day,
In the twilight zone, where dreams convene,
A world unseen, tranquil, serene.

Dreams of Coral Castles

In crystal grottos, soft and bright,
Coral castles rise at night,
Kings and queens of the sea so grand,
With jeweled crowns of ocean sand.

Colorful gardens of sea anemones,
Each gentle sway, a dance with the breeze,
In the depths, where wonders blend,
Every turn, a dream to send.

Turtles glide through the liquid grace,
In their wake, a tranquil trace,
Shells shimmer gently, a time-to-go,
In dreams of coral, love does flow.

Seahorses twirl in a delicate dance,
In this realm, they twinkle and prance,
Through coral gardens, they weave and glide,
With the sea's soft whispers, side by side.

Beneath the waves, where time is still,
In dreams of coral, hearts will fill,
For in each castle, a secret waits,
A world of wonder that time creates.

Quest for the Abyss

In the depths so dark and deep,
Mysteries hidden, secrets keep.
Whispers echo through the night,
We plunge forward, seeking light.

With each step, the shadows grow,
Ancient tales of woe bestow.
Hearts ignited, spirits bold,
In the abyss, the truth unfolds.

Creatures dwell in silence vast,
Guardians of the ocean's past.
We ride the currents, seek and find,
In the depths, our fates entwined.

Fathoms deep, where dreams will drift,
Every heartbeat, a precious gift.
In this quest, we lose control,
Yet the abyss can make us whole.

With courage bright, we face the tide,
In the dark, our fears must hide.
Together on this endless quest,
We search for truth, we find our rest.

Flavors of the Sea

Salt upon my lips so sweet,
Waves that dance beneath my feet.
Tastes of life in ocean's brine,
Savoring each drop divine.

From the depths, the treasures rise,
Colors twinkling, endless skies.
Sending whispers through the breeze,
Nature's bounty, fresh and free.

Crabs and clams, a feast we share,
Fishermen's nets filled with care.
Seagrass sways, the world alive,
In every bite, the sea's will thrive.

Underneath the sun's warm kiss,
Every flavor an ocean's bliss.
With each taste, the stories told,
In the sea, we find our gold.

Cradle of the Current

Rocked by waves, we gently sway,
In the cradle where dreams play.
Current's touch, soft as a sigh,
Carrying wishes, we drift by.

With the tide, we learn to flow,
Time embraced, as waters grow.
Stars above shine ever bright,
Guiding us through the velvet night.

Whispers of the ocean's lore,
As we sail for distant shore.
In the cradle, hearts will beat,
With the rhythm, pure and sweet.

Holding fast to every wave,
In this vessel, bold and brave.
We find solace in the stream,
In the current, live our dream.

Close your eyes, let worries flee,
In the water's harmony.
Cradle me, O gentle sea,
In your arms, I'm truly free.

Enchanted Thalassas

In the realm where dreams awaken,
Magic flows, the bonds unshaken.
Thalassas gleam, a sapphire hue,
A dance of waves, a world anew.

Mystical beings roam the deep,
In their dance, the secrets keep.
Serenade of the ocean's heart,
In enchanted realms, we take part.

Underneath the moon's soft glow,
Whispers of the tides will flow.
Each ripple tells a tale from old,
Of legends lost, and treasures bold.

To thalassas, our spirits soar,
Every tide reveals much more.
In their depths, we seek the quest,
To find our dreams, we are blessed.

With hearts in tune, we dive and swirl,
In the magic of this world.
Thalassas call, a siren's song,
In their embrace, we all belong.

Beneath Forgotten Ruins

In shadows deep, the stones decay,
Lost voices whisper secrets gray,
Beneath the arch of ancient stone,
Time's gentle hand has overgrown.

The vines embrace each crumbling wall,
While echoes of the past still call,
Once grand and bold, now silent plea,
In every crack, a history.

The mossy paths of faded light,
Guide weary souls through endless night,
Beneath the stars, a haunting tune,
Sings softly to the watching moon.

Forgotten tales in dust reside,
In twilight's hush, the dreams abide,
With every step, a story stirs,
Beneath the weight of time's soft purrs.

So stand awhile and breathe it in,
The life that was, where all begins,
In ruins clad in nature's grace,
A silent dance, an endless chase.

Mystical Waters

In twilight's glow, the waters gleam,
Reflecting whispers of a dream,
The surface shimmers, secrets flow,
In depthless realms where spirits go.

Beneath the waves, enchantments hide,
Where silver fish and shadows glide,
Each ripple sings of ancient lore,
Awakening what came before.

A tranquil calm, yet fierce and wild,
Where nature's heart remains a child,
Reviving songs of dusk and dawn,
In waters where the past moves on.

Through tangled reeds and lily pads,
The story weaves of joys and pads,
Mystical dreams in blue embrace,
Gently cradled in nature's grace.

So dare to dip your hand and feel,
The pulse beneath, a timeless reel,
For in the depths of every stream,
Lies hidden truth, and endless dream.

Forgotten Echoes

In silent halls where shadows dwell,
A thousand stories weave their spell,
Each echo carries whispers faint,
Of laughter, sorrow, love, and paint.

The floors are worn by fleeting feet,
As hearts once raced in rhythm sweet,
Forgotten now, the joy and pain,
In ghostly traces, love remains.

With every breath, the past revives,
In dusty corners, memory thrives,
A lingering song on evening air,
Recalls the moments, rich and rare.

The world outside may fade away,
But here, the echoes choose to stay,
In whispered tones, they softly glide,
Through time and space, they ever bide.

So listen close, let silence speak,
For in the quiet, spirits seek,
The timeless dance of life ere long,
In every note of whispered song.

Waterscapes of Time

On gentle waves, the moments drift,
Each ripple seems a precious gift,
Reflecting starlight's quiet gleam,
In waterscapes where dreamers dream.

With swaying reeds and drifting boats,
The world flows on, and silence floats,
A tapestry of shade and light,
Where memories dance in sweet delight.

The currents carve the tales untold,
Through valleys green and mountains bold,
A journey endless, wild and free,
In waters deep, eternity.

Beneath the azure canopy,
Time bends and sways, a melody,
Of laughter's echo, tears that dry,
As seasons pass, the years comply.

So cast your heart upon the stream,
And let it sail, as if a dream,
For in these waters, truth will show,
The beauty of the ebb and flow.

Waves of Tranquility

Softly they roll, the waves in the night,
Whispers of calm, in silver moonlight.
Each breath we take, with salt in the breeze,
Finding our peace, our hearts feel at ease.

The tide ebbs and flows, a dance so divine,
Starlight above, like a glittering vine.
Sand beneath feet, warm and so bright,
In this embrace, everything feels right.

Glistening shells, secrets they hold,
Stories of sailors, both timid and bold.
Nature's own rhythm, a lullaby sweet,
Here by the shore, where two worlds meet.

With each gentle crash, breath and release,
We're swept in the moment, enveloped in peace.
Troubles may linger, yet fade with the tide,
In waves of tranquility, we gently abide.

Fluid Footsteps

On shifting sands, we dance through the night,
Footprints like whispers, fading from sight.
Waves kiss our heels, a rhythmic embrace,
In this tranquil moment, we find our place.

Drifting like dreams, we flow with the tide,
Every pulse of the ocean, we cannot hide.
The moon casts a glow, guiding our way,
Fluid footsteps linger, then swiftly decay.

Carried by currents, lost in the foam,
Each gentle wave, beckoning us home.
With hearts open wide, we let go the past,
In fluid footsteps, our spirits are cast.

Resonating echoes, under the stars,
Embracing the sea, with its sweet memoirs.
Each step is a journey, every splash a song,
In this dance of water, we truly belong.

A Symphony of Fishes

Beneath the waves, a world concealed,
A tapestry of life, harmonies revealed.
Colors entwined, a dance of delight,
Fishes play music, in depths out of sight.

Swirling through corals, with graceful finesse,
A symphony rising, a vibrant caress.
Each fin tells a story, each scale shines with grace,
Together they weave, in this fluid space.

In echoes of laughter, the bubbles ascend,
Mirroring rhythms, as currents blend.
A treasure of voices, serene and profound,
In the ocean's embrace, our hearts feel unbound.

Nature's own orchestra, in blue hues and gold,
Every note played, a tale to be told.
As day turns to twilight, the waters aglow,
In this symphony of fishes, we let our hearts flow.

Lost in the Currents

Caught in the flow, where the waters collide,
The currents are strong, deeper than pride.
Drifting we stumble, yet find our way,
Lost in these waters, where dreams come to play.

The rush of the stream, like whispers of fate,
Leading us onward, it's never too late.
In eddies we twirl, with laughter and fear,
Riding the waves, together we steer.

Swells rise like mountains, then dip low and deep,
While tides murmur secrets, the ocean does keep.
Yet here in the wild, we're no longer alone,
In the dance of the currents, our spirits have grown.

With water around us, we cannot despair,
Each twist and each turn, a chance to declare.
That lost we may be, on this journey so grand,
In the depths of the currents, together we stand.

Beneath the Surface

Beneath the waves, secrets hide,
A world where shadows silently bide.
Coral gardens glow and gleam,
In the twilight's soft, whispered dream.

Creatures dance the ocean's tune,
Underneath the watchful moon.
Silent whispers drift and sway,
Guiding lost souls on their way.

Mysteries wrapped in gentle foam,
Where marine hearts call their home.
Visions flicker in watery light,
Chasing wonders throughout the night.

Echoes of the deep resound,
Where ancient trails can be found.
Beneath the surface, life persists,
In a realm that pulses and twists.

The depths conceal, the currents share,
A playground of life beyond compare.
So dive with grace into the blue,
And feel the magic echo true.

Whispering Tides

Whispering tides call out to me,
In harmony with the endless sea.
Their gentle lull, a sweet embrace,
In every wave, a timeless trace.

Moonlit dances, secrets shared,
Every tide knows how I've cared.
Soft sands shift beneath my feet,
In this ocean, life feels complete.

Shells and stones tell stories bold,
In their silence, wisdom told.
The seafoam kisses the shore's line,
In every touch, your heart is mine.

Breezes carry your laughter near,
A melody I long to hear.
Whispering tides, forever flow,
In their embrace, true love will grow.

As dusk falls, the stars ignite,
In the vast expanse of night.
Whispering tides, so sincere,
Reveal my dreams, forever near.

Shadows in the Deep

Shadows linger in the sea,
Dancing softly, wild and free.
Mysteries wrapped in darkened shades,
Where light struggles, and hope fades.

Creatures glide through midnight's lane,
In the depths, where dreams remain.
Echoed calls of the lost and found,
Resound softly in their sound.

Waves whisper secrets long since gone,
Drawing forth tales to gaze upon.
Tales of longing and of fear,
In the deep where none draw near.

Time stands still in ocean grave,
Among the shadows, we all crave.
Ghostly figures, fleeting grace,
Forever haunting this sacred place.

Yet in this darkness, light will break,
As dawn approaches, hearts awake.
Shadows in the deep retreat,
Giving way to life's own beat.

Dreams of the Abyss

Dreams of the abyss swirl and dive,
Deep in the silence, echoes thrive.
Where the dark and light intertwine,
Creating visions, pure and divine.

From solemn depths, pure whispers rise,
Carried gently 'neath starlit skies.
Tales of longing, hope, and dread,
In the vastness, where few have tread.

In the abyss, a calling stirs,
A longing tied with gentle spurs.
Each heartbeat dances, softly pulses,
In the depths, where the soul convulses.

Waves of dreams lap at the shore,
A realm of depths forevermore.
Lost in currents, my spirit roams,
Finding solace in ocean's homes.

In these dreams, the abyss holds sway,
Guiding my heart, come what may.
Embracing the dark, I will find bliss,
In the depths of the abyss, where shadows kiss.

Radiance Below

In the depths where shadows play,
Light dances in a gentle sway.
Colors swirl in a silent flow,
This is the magic of radiance below.

Fish dart by with gleaming scales,
Through the dark where silence hails.
The sea a canvas, rich and bright,
Nature's art in the still of night.

Coral blooms in vibrant hue,
A hidden world, alive and true.
Secrets stir within the tide,
Where mystery and beauty glide.

Echoes linger, soft and sweet,
In this realm where wonders meet.
The ocean sings a timeless song,
In the depths where we belong.

What lies beneath, a treasure trove,
In silence deep, the heart can rove.
Lost in waves, we find our way,
In the radiance, we long to stay.

Crystal Caverns

In the heart of the earth, they gleam,
Crystal caverns, where shadows dream.
Nature's breath in a glimmering vault,
Beauty emerges without a fault.

Rays of light through facets shine,
Illuminating paths divine.
Stalactites hanging like jewels rare,
In this magic, we're unaware.

Whispers echo in the still,
Stories told by the ancient thrill.
Values found in every stone,
In the caverns, we are not alone.

Colors dance in the cool, damp air,
A secret world beyond compare.
Beneath our feet, the wonders lie,
In crystal caverns, we can't deny.

Let your spirit wander free,
In the depths of eternity.
Here in silence, hearts entwine,
In crystal caverns, love will shine.

Whispering Kelp

Under waves where waters sway,
Whispering kelp's soft ballet.
Gentle strokes in liquid green,
A dance of life, a tranquil scene.

Tendrils sway in rhythmic grace,
Inviting fish to join the chase.
Sunlight filtering down from above,
In every ripple, a tale of love.

A hidden world at nature's feet,
Murmurs echo, soft and sweet.
The sway of seaweed, a lullaby,
In the depths, where hearts can fly.

Kelp forests growing tall and wide,
A shelter where the small ones hide.
In the currents, life unfolds,
Whispering tales that nature holds.

Dive beneath the azure waves,
Where every pulse the ocean saves.
For in this realm of embrace and help,
We find our peace in whispering kelp.

The Language of Waves

Listen close to the ocean's song,
The language of waves, so vast and strong.
Each crash a word, each sigh a theme,
In liquid rhythm, we find our dream.

Voices call from the distant shore,
Songs of seagulls, an ancient lore.
With every roll, the sea imparts,
A melody that stirs our hearts.

Gentle lapping, a soothing sound,
In the ebb and flow, life's joys abound.
Secrets whisper through salty air,
A communion found, so rare, so rare.

The tides compose a symphony,
Through every wave, there's harmony.
In each crest, the world's embrace,
With every break, we find our place.

Dance upon the shifting sand,
Feel the language, hand in hand.
For the sea speaks in joyous raves,
And we listen to the language of waves.

Tributes of the Current

In the river's flow we find,
Stories of the hearts entwined.
Each ripple sings a whispered tale,
As waters dance, and dreams set sail.

Stones beneath, they hold our past,
Memories formed, forever cast.
With each wave, a soft embrace,
Nature's hand, a gentle grace.

Through time's hands, we see it thrive,
Time's sweet current keeps hope alive.
Tributes rise, as waters part,
A symphony, the river's heart.

The currents run, relentless, deep,
Guarding secrets, lessons keep.
In their flow, our spirits soar,
Grateful for the tales they pour.

In every bend, a new surprise,
Nature paints with vibrant skies.
Tributes of the current flow,
In silent whispers, wisdom grows.

Shimmers of Light

In the dawn's first gentle glow,
Whispers dance, the world aglow.
Threads of gold, they weave and spin,
Inviting warmth, where hope begins.

Caught in dewdrops, glimmers gleam,
Nature's jewels, pure as a dream.
Each ray casts shadows, rich and wide,
Embracing all that dwells inside.

The twilight hues, a canvas bright,
Stars awaken, sharing light.
In every flicker, stories weave,
A tender promise, we believe.

With every evening's sweet embrace,
Shimmers spark a gentle grace.
Life ignites in colors bold,
A treasure trove of tales untold.

In the moon's soft, silver glow,
Whispers float, as breezes blow.
Shimmers of light, pure and free,
Illuminate our journey's spree.

Soul of the Sea

In oceans deep, where dreams reside,
The soul of the sea, vast and wide.
Waves that rise and fall in time,
Chanting songs, a rhythmic rhyme.

Whispers from the depths below,
Secrets only currents know.
Beneath the surface, life abounds,
In harmony with soothing sounds.

Islands call, a siren's song,
Echoes rich where heartbeats throng.
Every tide, a cycle true,
The sea's embrace, forever new.

In twilight's hues, reflections glow,
A myriad of tides in flow.
The soul of the sea ignites the night,
In every splash, a dance of light.

With each dawn, the horizon gleams,
Fishing boats, a dance of dreams.
The soul of the sea, wild and free,
A timeless voyage, you and me.

Horizons of Blue

Endless skies, a cerulean hue,
Where dreams are born, and hopes rise too.
The gentle breeze whispers to me,
In vast reflections, I feel free.

Mountains high, they touch the skies,
In splendor pure, the spirit flies.
Horizons meet, where land takes flight,
A canvas brushed with morning light.

In depths of oceans, blue unfolds,
Stories of the brave retold.
Each wave may crash, but still it soars,
An endless dance on distant shores.

With every glance, horizons call,
Inviting us to risk it all.
In shades of blue, we find our way,
Guided forth through night and day.

Horizons of blue, vast and grand,
Hold the dreams of every land.
Together we'll chase the sky's embrace,
In the beauty of this boundless space.

The Beauty of the Deep

In the silence, colors gleam,
Coral castles, a vibrant dream.
Gentle creatures sway and flow,
In the depths, wonders glow.

Echoes of whispers, soft and clear,
Dancing shadows, drawing near.
Fins like ribbons in the sea,
Nature's art, wild and free.

Rippling currents, soft caress,
A tranquil world, pure finesse.
Mystic realms, life's ballet,
In the deep, we drift away.

Sunlight sparkles, beams of gold,
Secrets of the sea unfold.
Every wave, a timeless song,
In the depths, we all belong.

Starlit skies from below to view,
Gentle tides, a love so true.
Embrace the deep, let it seep,
In its heart, our souls we'll keep.

Subaquatic Ballet

Fins flutter gracefully in the blue,
A dance of life, so fresh and new.
Each twist and turn, a silent cheer,
Underwater, nothing to fear.

Sea turtles glide in calm ballet,
With every move, they sway and play.
Jellyfish float, like dreams untold,
In this realm, beauty unfolds.

Crabs in rhythm, pinch and scuttle,
Starfish twirl, without a muddle.
Seahorses entwined in embrace,
Together, they twirl in endless space.

Fish in schools, a vibrant hue,
Dancing to melodies, ancient and true.
Amidst the kelp, a soft ballet,
Life in motion, forever in sway.

Currents swirl, a gentle guide,
In the deep, where dreams reside.
Let the dance take you away,
In the sea's arms, forever stay.

Journey Through the Blue

Beneath the waves, we take a dive,
Where magic flows, and creatures thrive.
A journey starts with every breath,
Into the blue, away from death.

Dolphins play in arcs of grace,
In this vast, enchanting space.
With every stroke, the world expands,
Following dreams with open hands.

Anemones dance with lights aglow,
As currents swirl and softly flow.
Bright parrotfish, with colors bold,
In this realm, stories unfold.

Explorers of the ocean's deep,
In the whispers of the tide, we leap.
Each bend reveals a new delight,
In the blue, darkness meets the light.

We drift along the ocean's song,
Where every heartbeat feels like long.
Journey through, don't hesitate,
In the blue, we'll resonate.

The Laughter of Shells

On the shore, a chorus sings,
Shells like jewels, ocean's bling.
Every whisper a memory,
Echoes of waves, wild and free.

Seashell laughter, soft and sweet,
Tales of journeys from the deep.
Gather them close, treasures divine,
Each a story, unique in line.

Curly conchs and smooth abalone,
Part of nature's vast symphony.
Hear the tales they softly tell,
Of distant shores where they once dwell.

In the sand, we find our peace,
With every shell, all worries cease.
The laughter of shells, a gentle balm,
Bringing comfort, keeping calm.

Let the beach be our escape,
In every shell, a world takes shape.
The laughter of seashells, pure delight,
Guiding us through day and night.

Flows of Forgotten Remembrance

Whispers drift on silent streams,
Echoes of what once had been,
Memories wrapped in gentle dreams,
Time slips through our hands serene.

Faded images in the mist,
Stories linger in the air,
Moments sweet, though hard to twist,
In the heart, forever share.

Footsteps rest on paths of gold,
Each token marks a place we knew,
Tales of warmth and love retold,
Cherished faces shine anew.

Shadows dance beneath the trees,
Dancing leaves in twilight's hue,
Softly carried by the breeze,
Lost forever, yet so true.

Through the rivers deep and wide,
Rippling time flows endlessly,
In the currents, hearts confide,
Embracing all that we can see.

Cerulean Secrets

Beneath the waves, a world unfolds,
Secrets held in rippling blue,
Whispers drift in currents bold,
Mysteries await for me and you.

Coral castles gleam so bright,
Guardians of the ocean's lore,
Softly glowing in the night,
Hiding treasures on the floor.

Seafoam dances, light and free,
Ebbing rhythms call us near,
In the depths, we long to see,
Every story, every tear.

Fishes swirl in vibrant hues,
Painting stories with their flight,
Cerulean depths, like a muse,
Inspiring dreams of pure delight.

As the tides, they rise and fall,
Nature's pulse, a timeless beat,
In the silence, hear the call,
Cerulean secrets, bittersweet.

Coral Kingdoms

In the heart of azure seas,
Coral kingdoms rise and swell,
Home to life that swims with ease,
In the depths, their stories tell.

Colors burst in vibrant shades,
A tapestry of life displayed,
In these realms, the magic wades,
Nature's art, forever played.

Gentle waves caress the shore,
Tales are written in the sand,
Whispers of the ocean's lore,
Holding dreams that still withstand.

Beneath the surface, wonder sleeps,
Every corner holds a tale,
Where the pulse of nature keeps,
And the heart of beauty trails.

Coral kingdoms, wild and free,
Basking in the ocean's grace,
In their depths, we long to be,
Wanders lost in time and space.

Rippled Reflections

Still waters mirror the sky,
Ripples dance with a gentle sigh,
In the silence, secrets flow,
Reflections tell us all we know.

Echoes linger upon the lake,
Whispers weave through bending reeds,
Nature's breath, a soft mistake,
In the calm, the heart simply feeds.

Shadows play on twilight's face,
Rippling memories swirl beneath,
Each soft touch, an embrace of grace,
Floating dreams, a perfect sheath.

As the stars begin to shine,
The water sparkles in the night,
In this moment, your hand in mine,
Rippling reflections feel so right.

Life's a canvas, painted clear,
Nature's brush strokes guide our way,
In each ripple, love draws near,
As reflections softly sway.

Milton Keynes UK
Ingram Content Group UK Ltd.
UKHW022239280824
447491UK00010B/281